The Usborne
Children's Bible

The Usborne Children's Bible

Retold by Heather Amery
Illustrated by Linda Edwards

Designed by Amanda Barlow
Edited by Jenny Tyler

The Old Testament

The New Testament

How the World Began

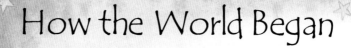

Long, long ago, there was no world, no sky, no sun or stars, not even any day or night. There was only swirling water in a huge dark empty space. Then God made light and this was the very first day.

On the second day, God made the sky. Under the sky was nothing but water. God collected the water together to make the seas. Between the seas was dry land. God then ordered all kinds of plants and trees to grow on the land. That was the third day.

The next day, God put the sun in the sky to shine during the day and the moon to shine at night. On the fifth day, God said that all kinds of creatures should swim in the seas and all kinds of birds should fly in the sky. He blessed them, told them to have their

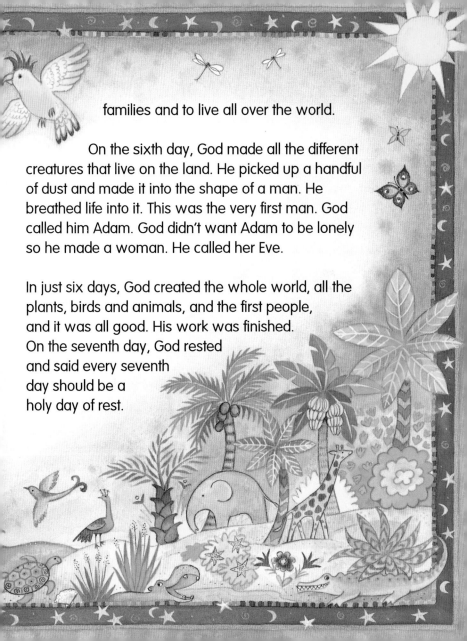

families and to live all over the world.

On the sixth day, God made all the different creatures that live on the land. He picked up a handful of dust and made it into the shape of a man. He breathed life into it. This was the very first man. God called him Adam. God didn't want Adam to be lonely so he made a woman. He called her Eve.

In just six days, God created the whole world, all the plants, birds and animals, and the first people, and it was all good. His work was finished. On the seventh day, God rested and said every seventh day should be a holy day of rest.

Adam and Eve

Adam and Eve lived in a beautiful garden God made specially for them. It was full of flowers and fruit trees. God told Adam he could eat the fruit from any of the trees, except the ones that grew on the Tree of Knowledge of Good and Evil. If he ate that, he would die.

Adam and Eve were very happy in the garden. There were sparkling rivers and every kind of animal and bird. Adam and Eve made friends with them all. Sometimes, God walked in the garden with Adam and Eve on warm summer evenings and talked to them.

A snake lived in the Garden. One sleepy afternoon, it slithered up to Eve and whispered in her ear. "Did God say you could eat the fruit of all the trees?" it asked.

"Yes," replied Eve, "except the fruit on the Tree of Knowledge in the middle of the Garden. If we touch or eat those, we shall die."

"You won't die," whispered the snake. "God knows that if you do eat it, you will become as wise as gods."

Eve walked slowly to the special tree. The fruit looked delicious. She picked one and took a big bite out of it. When Adam came up, she gave him the rest of the fruit to eat.

Then Adam and Eve looked at each other and saw for the first time that they had no clothes on. They felt very shy. They rushed away and sewed leaves together to make clothes before they could look at each other again.

That evening, God walked in the Garden. "Adam," He called, "where are you?"

"I'm here. I'm hiding from you because I know now that I was naked," said Adam.

"How do you know? Have you eaten the fruit I told you not to touch?" asked God.

"Eve gave it to me," said Adam.

"Why did you disobey me?" God asked Eve.

"The snake told me to," said Eve.

"Because you have disobeyed me, you must leave my Garden," said God. "You will have to work hard to grow food. The ground will be rough and stony and full of thorns and thistles. And when you grow old, you will die."

God watched Adam and Eve go out of the Garden. They had to begin their new, hard life on Earth. They were very miserable.

God sent an angel with a flaming sword to guard the Garden of Eden so that no one could ever go into it again.

11

Noah and his Ark

After many years, God looked at the world he had made and was sad. The people were bad, they hurt each other and did not listen to Him any more. God decided to flood the whole world so that everybody in it would drown.

There was just one man who loved God and obeyed Him. His name was Noah. God said to Noah, "You must build an ark, a huge boat, so I can save your family and all the creatures on Earth. I will tell you exactly how big it must be."

Noah did what God told him. He cut down trees and collected all the things he needed. Then he began to build his ark. His three sons helped him. They marked out the shape of the ark on the ground and made a wooden frame. Then they covered it with wood and put tar on the inside and outside to make the ark waterproof.

After months and months of hard work, it was finished. It had three decks, a door in the side and a roof, just as God had told Noah to build it. Noah and his family loaded the ark with food and water for themselves and for all the creatures.

Just as they were carrying on the last load, huge clouds drifted across the sky, blocking out the sun. Noah looked up and a few drops of rain fell on his head. Then he looked toward the hills. A huge procession of creatures was walking, trotting, creeping, slithering or flying in an endless line. There were two of every kind of animal and bird in the world. Noah stared at them. "I didn't know there were so many," he said. As he watched, they filed into the ark. There was just enough room for them all. Noah and his wife and his three sons and their wives went in too, and God closed the door after them.

Then it began to rain. It rained and rained for forty days and nights. Slowly the water flooded the ground and the ark floated away on a huge new sea, with everyone safely inside.

Outside, the water rose until it covered the very tops of the mountains, and everybody and everything left on the Earth was drowned in the flood.

For months and months the ark tossed on the waves of a huge empty sea. At last, the rain stopped and the water began to go down a little. Noah opened a window and sent off a raven. "Go and find some dry land," he said. The raven flew a very long way but it couldn't find any dry land.

Later Noah sent off a dove. It flew away but came back again. Noah waited a week and sent the dove off again. This time, it came back with a twig in its beak. "That means there is dry land and things are growing again," said Noah.

After another week, he sent off the dove again but, this time, it didn't come back. Noah lifted off a cover on the ark and looked out. At last, he could see land. Noah opened the door of the ark, and everyone rushed out. The land was dry and the sun was shining.

"Spread out all over the Earth and have your families," God said to Noah and to all the creatures.

Noah looked up and thanked God for saving them from the terrible flood. In the sky was a rainbow. "That is my sign," said God. "I promise I will never flood the whole Earth again."

Abraham and Sarah

Abraham was a rich man who lived in the city of Haran with his wife Sarah. They were both old and, to their great sadness, had never had any children.

One day, God said to Abraham, "I want you to go to the land of Canaan. There I will make you the father of a great nation."

Abraham didn't understand what God meant, but he always did what God told him to do. Soon he started out for Canaan with Sarah, his nephew Lot and his wife, and all his servants and his herds of sheep and goats. It was a very long journey but, at last, they reached the new land and put up their tents.

At first there was plenty of grass and water for Abraham's herds of sheep and goats and for Lot's herds as well. But, as the years passed, the herds grew bigger and bigger and there wasn't enough food for them all.

"It's time for us to part," Abraham said to Lot. "You can choose where you want to go."

"I'll go down to the valley. There's plenty of good grass and water there," said Lot.

"I'll stay here on the hills," said Abraham, although he knew the food and water wasn't so good. Lot and his wife said goodbye to Abraham and Sarah and led their sheep down to the valley. God again promised Abraham that He would make his family into a great nation.

One hot afternoon some years later, when Abraham was sitting in his tent, he saw three men crossing the hills. When they came nearer, he went to meet them.

"Come to my tent," Abraham said to the strangers. "You can wash and rest there, and have a meal."

Sarah and the servants made fresh bread, roasted some meat on the fire and gave the three men bowls of milk and cheese. When the feast was over, one of the men said, "We have a message from God for you.

You and Sarah will have a baby boy."

"We're both much too old to have children," laughed
Sarah. But the months went by and Sarah
gave birth to a son. She called him
Isaac. Abraham and Sarah were
delighted that they had a child at last.
And Abraham remembered
that God had told
him he would be
the father of a
great nation.

Isaac and Rebecca

Isaac, the son of Abraham and Sarah, grew up a strong and tall young man. Sarah had died and Abraham decided it was time for Isaac to have a wife. But it had to be a girl from their own people who lived far away from Canaan.

Abraham said to a servant, "Go to my brother Nahor to choose a wife for Isaac and bring her here."

"If she doesn't want to come, shall I take Isaac to her?" asked the man.

"No, Isaac must stay here. God promised this land to my family,"

said Abraham. "She must come and live with us here."

The servant began his long journey with some other servants, taking ten camels and presents for the girl and her family. At last he stopped at a well outside the city walls. It was late in the afternoon and soon the girls would come to the well to fill their water jars.

The servant said a prayer to God. "Please help me find a wife for Isaac. I'll say to one of the girls, 'Please give me a drink from your water jar.' If she says, 'Yes, and I will also give water to your camels,' let her be the right wife for Isaac."

Before he finished his prayer, the servant looked up and saw a beautiful girl

walking to the well. After she had filled her jar, he asked for water. She gave him the jar and, after he had a long drink, she filled her jar again and again with water for his camels.

The servant knew this was the sign he had prayed for. He gave the girl a gold ring and two gold bracelets. "Tell me who you are," he said. "May we spend the night in your father's house?"

"My name is Rebecca and my grandfather's name is Nahor. We have plenty of room for you and food for your camels," said the girl.

The servant thanked God for leading him straight to Abraham's family.

Rebecca ran to her house. She told her family about the man she had met at the well and showed them the presents he had given her. Laban, her brother, went back to the well and asked the servant and other men to come to the house.

After the camels were fed for the night, everyone sat down to a good meal. But the servant would not start eating until he had told Rebecca's family why he had come.

He told them about Abraham and Sarah and their son, Isaac, and how he had asked God to help him choose the right girl at the well. Then he asked her family if they would let Rebecca go back to Canaan with him to be Isaac's wife.

Rebecca's family saw it was the will of God and agreed that Rebecca should go. Abraham's servant gave presents of jewels to Rebecca and presents to her mother and brother. Then they feasted to celebrate the engagement.

Abraham's servant wanted to go home at once and Rebecca agreed to go with him. The next morning, the men loaded up the camels. Rebecca said goodbye to her family and began the long journey to Canaan.

It was evening when, at last, they reached Abraham's tent. Isaac was out in the fields and saw the camels coming. He went to meet them and the servant told him everything that had happened. Isaac looked at the beautiful girl who had come so far to be his bride. He soon married her, and he loved her.

Joseph and his Wonderful Coat

Jacob, Isaac's son, was a rich farmer who lived in Canaan. He had twelve sons and, although he loved them all, he loved his son Joseph most of all. He gave Joseph a wonderful coat. Joseph strutted around in it, thinking himself very grand. His brothers were jealous. They hated him because Joseph said he dreamed he would be much more important than them.

One day, Jacob sent Joseph out to a far valley to his brothers and their flocks of sheep and goats. When his brothers saw Joseph coming, one said, "Let's kill him. We could tell our father that a wild animal has eaten him."

But another brother said, "We mustn't kill him. Let's put him into that pit." Just then, some merchants passed by on their way to Egypt. The brothers sold Joseph to them as a slave and the merchants led him away. The brothers put goat's blood on Joseph's coat and went home to their father.

"We found this coat. Is it Joseph's?" one brother asked him. Jacob recognized the coat and, when he saw the blood on it, he thought Joseph was dead. He was very sad.

The merchants took Joseph to Egypt and sold him as a slave to Potiphar, the captain of the King's guard. Joseph worked hard and soon Potiphar put him in charge of his household. For a time, all went well, but Potiphar's wife wanted to make trouble for Joseph. She told Potiphar, "That Joseph has been very rude to me."

It wasn't true, but Potiphar was angry with Joseph. He had him put in prison. God had made Joseph very good at telling people what their dreams meant and he explained the other prisoners' dreams to them.

After Joseph had been in prison for two years, the King of Egypt had a strange dream. He asked his wise men what it meant, but no one could explain it. Then someone remembered that Joseph was good at dreams. He was brought to the King. The King told Joseph his dream.

Joseph said, "Your dream means that for seven years there will be good harvests with lots of food for everyone. But then there will be seven years when the harvests are bad and many people will be hungry, even starving."

The King was so pleased with Joseph, he put him in charge of all the stores of food in Egypt. For seven years, there were good harvests and Joseph made sure the extra grain was stored away. When the seven bad years came, Joseph had plenty of food to sell to the people.

Far away in Canaan, Joseph's father and brothers grew short of food. Jacob said, "You must go to Egypt to buy grain. They have plenty". Ten brothers began the journey, leaving the youngest, Benjamin, behind.

In Egypt, the brothers asked the governor if they could buy food. They didn't know he was their brother Joseph, but Joseph knew at once they were his brothers. He spoke sternly and asked them about their father and Benjamin.

He said, "I'll sell you food but when you come again, you must bring Benjamin with you. I'll keep your brother Simeon here until you come back."

The brothers started for home. On the way, they opened the sacks of grain they had bought and found the money they had paid to Joseph. They were very frightened. "God is punishing us for selling Joseph," the brothers said. They didn't know Joseph had told his servants to put it there.

After a while, Jacob and his sons had eaten all the grain. They had to go back to Egypt to buy more, but this time they took Benjamin with them. Again, they asked Joseph to sell them food and still they didn't know he was their brother. Joseph ordered his servants to give them a meal, making sure Benjamin had plenty to eat.

The next morning, the eleven brothers started for home.

On the way, Joseph's guards caught up with them and opened the sacks of grain. In Benjamin's sack was Joseph's silver cup. Joseph had told his guards to hide it there. He wanted to test his brothers.

The guards marched the scared brothers back to Egypt and took them to Joseph. "You may go home," he said, "but you must leave Benjamin here with me."

The brothers were very upset. "Please let us take Benjamin with us," they begged. "Our father has already lost one son. If he loses Benjamin, it will break his heart. Let one of us stay here instead of Benjamin." Joseph knew then that his brothers had changed and were sorry for what they had done to him long ago.

"I am Joseph, your brother whom you sold as a slave," Joseph cried. "But it was God who sent me to Egypt so that I could save you from dying of hunger. God promised Abraham that the nation he founded would be safe. Go back to my father and bring him here, with all your family and your animals. I will give you good land and we will all live well and happily in Egypt."

Moses in the Bulrushes

Many years after Joseph died, Egypt had a new King who was very cruel to Joseph's family, the Hebrews, who lived in Egypt. He made them work as slaves. They were forced to make bricks of mud to build great cities and temples for the King and to work on the land.

The Hebrews worked hard from early morning until late at night, watched over by Egyptian guards, and they were beaten if they tried to rest.

There were so many Hebrews in Egypt by this time that the King was frightened they would rebel against him and seize his throne. So he made a new law and ordered his soldiers to kill all the Hebrew baby boys as soon as they were born.

One Hebrew mother managed to hide her new baby son, called Moses, until he was three months old. But as he grew older, she was afraid the Egyptian soldiers would hear him crying, find him and then kill him.

One day, she picked up Moses and hurried secretly down to the river bank. There she made a basket out of reeds and covered the outside with tar to make it waterproof. When the basket was finished, she put Moses in it. He was fast asleep. She put the basket gently down on the water and pushed it out on the great Nile river.

Moses's sister was hiding in the reeds. She watched the basket float away down the river. She followed it, walking along the bank to see where it would go.

A little farther along the bank, the Egyptian Princess came down to the river to swim with her servants. She saw the

basket floating on the water between
the reeds.

"Bring that basket here," she ordered one of her maids.
The maid picked up the basket and brought it to her.

When the Princess saw the baby, she said, "That must be
a Hebrew boy." At that moment, Moses woke up and
cried a little. The Princess felt so sorry for him, she
decided to keep him.

Moses's sister watched, hidden in the reeds.

She saw what happened. She ran to the Princess. "Do you want a Hebrew nurse to look after the baby for you?" she asked.

"Yes," said the Princess. "Bring one to me," she ordered.

Moses's sister ran quickly to her mother and told her what had happened. Then she led her mother to the Princess. "Take this baby away and look after him for me. I will pay you well," said the Princess.

Moses's mother very happily took her baby son home and looked after him. He was safe now. He stayed with his mother and the rest of his family until he was old enough to go back to the Princess. Then his mother took Moses to the palace.

"He is my son now," said the Princess.

Moses grew up in the palace with the Princess. He was treated just as if he was an Egyptian prince, but he never forgot that he was really a Hebrew.

Moses Leads his
People out of Egypt

Moses was an important man in Egypt, but he was very unhappy when he saw how badly the Egyptian masters treated their Hebrew slaves. One day, he saw an Egyptian whip a Hebrew man. Moses killed the Egyptian but someone saw him, and Moses knew the King would hear about it. The King would have Moses put to death.

Moses escaped into the desert and lived there for a long time. One day, he saw a bush on fire but it wasn't burning up. As he went closer, God spoke to him.

"You must go to Egypt," said God. "Take your brother Aaron with you and ask the King to let the Hebrews leave Egypt. He will not agree but I will make him. Then all the world will know that I am God. You will lead the Hebrews to a land where they will be free and have plenty to eat."

33

Moses didn't want to go, but he knew he must obey God. He and Aaron went to the King and asked him to set the Hebrews free.

The King was very angry. He said he wouldn't let the Hebrews go, and made them work even harder. Moses was in despair. He asked God to help him. Then he went back to the King again.

Moses warned the King that if he did not let the Hebrews leave Egypt, God would make terrible things happen. But still the King refused. Then the terrible things began. First, the river turned red and no one could drink the water.

A week later, thousands of frogs swarmed out of the river and into all the Egyptian houses. Then there were clouds of horrible flies which filled the King's palace and all the houses, except the Hebrews' houses. But the King wouldn't let the Hebrews go.

Then the animals began to die and the Egyptian people were ill with horrible sores on their bodies. After that, there were terrible storms.

Hail flattened the crops and great clouds of locusts ate up what was left. But still the King would not let the Hebrews go.

The worst thing of all was when the eldest child of every

Egyptian family died one night. God had told Moses what the Hebrews should do to be safe. Every family killed a lamb and put a little blood on the doorposts of the house. Then they roasted the lamb and ate it with flat bread and herbs. God said the Hebrews should always remember when death passed over them, and keep it as a special feast day.

At last, the King said the Hebrews could go. The next day they left Egypt, following a column of smoke during the day and a column of fire at night, sent by God.

Then the King changed his mind. He sent his army racing in chariots after the Hebrews. The Hebrews saw them coming and were terrified. In front of them was the Red Sea and behind them were the King's soldiers.

Moses told them not to be afraid because God would help them. He pointed across the water and a strong east wind, sent by God, blew away the water making a dry path for them to hurry across. But when the Egyptian soldiers tried to follow them, the sea rushed back and the soldiers were all drowned. The Hebrews were free, at last, to go to the land which God had promised them.

Moses in the Desert

Led by Moses, the people walked for weeks across the desert to their new land. They soon forgot they had been slaves in Egypt. They were hungry and grumbled. "We should have stayed in Egypt. We had plenty of food there. Remember all the good things we had to eat," they said. "We had meat and bread, melons, onions and cucumbers. It would be better to be in Egypt than dying of hunger in the desert."

God heard the people grumbling and said to Moses, "Tell the people I will give them meat to eat every evening and bread every morning."

That evening, flocks of birds, called quails, landed on the people's tents and were easy to catch. So that night everyone ate roasted quail. In the morning, the ground was covered with small white seeds. They looked just like frost. The people collected them, ground them into flour, made it into bread and baked it. They called it "manna" because it was food which came from Heaven. It was very good to eat and tasted like honey.

Every day, the same thing happened. The people ate bread made of manna in the morning and roasted quails in the evening. On the sixth day, Moses told them to collect enough food for two days. This was so they wouldn't have to work on the seventh day, the Sabbath, but would keep it as a holy day of rest.

Now the people had plenty to eat, but soon they grew short of water. They were thirsty and started to grumble again. "We should have stayed in Egypt rather than die of thirst in the desert," they said.

Moses prayed to God. "What shall I do with these people?" he asked. "They are almost ready to kill me."

"Take your stick and walk on ahead of the people. Then strike a rock with your stick," God said to Moses. Moses did as God told him and when he struck the rock, a great stream of water gushed out. There was plenty of fresh water for everyone.

God looked after the Hebrew people all the years they lived in the desert. He sent them food when they were hungry and water when they were thirsty.

Moses and the Laws of God

Moses led the people across the desert to Mount Sinai, as God told him to do. For weeks they trekked across the hot, dry land but God always sent them food and water. At last, they stopped and camped at the foot of the mountain. Moses climbed up to pray to God.

God told him that the people must be ready for Him to speak to them. Then the sky grew dark, thunder rolled and lightning flashed. Smoke and fire gushed out of the top of the mountain and the ground shook. There was the sound of a loud trumpet. The people were terrified; they knew that God was near.

Then God spoke to Moses out of the fire and smoke. He gave him ten laws that the people must always keep.

"I am your God. You must have no other gods but Me.

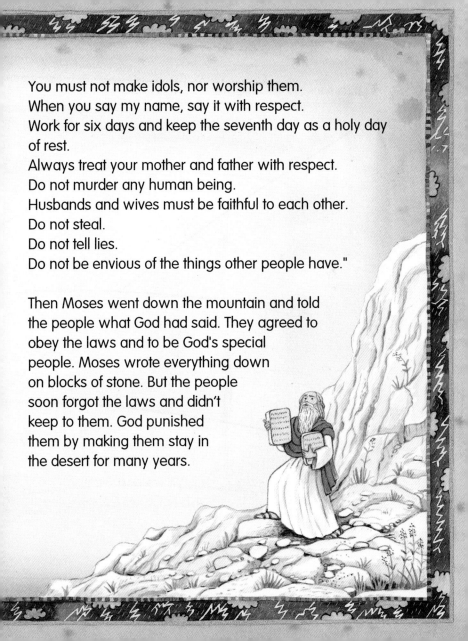

You must not make idols, nor worship them.
When you say my name, say it with respect.
Work for six days and keep the seventh day as a holy day of rest.
Always treat your mother and father with respect.
Do not murder any human being.
Husbands and wives must be faithful to each other.
Do not steal.
Do not tell lies.
Do not be envious of the things other people have."

Then Moses went down the mountain and told the people what God had said. They agreed to obey the laws and to be God's special people. Moses wrote everything down on blocks of stone. But the people soon forgot the laws and didn't keep to them. God punished them by making them stay in the desert for many years.

Joshua and Jericho

After the people had lived for forty years in the desert, Moses died. Joshua now led the people to the land God had promised them. They crossed the Jordan river and reached the city of Jericho. God told Joshua that He would give it to them.

Joshua looked at Jericho's enormous stone walls and huge wooden gates. Then God told him what to do. Every day for six days, Joshua marched with soldiers once around the city. Behind them came seven priests who blew their trumpets. No one else made a sound.

On the seventh day, they marched around the city seven times and when the priests blew their trumpets, they all shouted as loudly as they could. Then, with a great crash, the walls fell down and the soldiers rushed into Jericho. They took all the treasure they could find. This was the people's first victory in Canaan and Joshua soon became famous. Over the years, the people settled in Canaan and grew to be a very strong nation because God was with them.

Samson, a Mighty Man

Manoah and his wife had been married for many years, but were sad because they had no children. One day, God sent an angel to Manoah's wife to tell her she would have a son. He would save her people, the Israelites, from the Philistines who ruled over them.

Manoah and his wife were delighted. When the boy was born, they called him Samson. They never cut his hair to show that he belonged to God. Samson grew up to be a huge, immensely strong man. One day, when he was walking through a vineyard, a lion roared at him. He grabbed the lion and killed it with his bare hands. Samson knew then that God had made him especially strong for the work he had to do.

He fought the Philistines whenever he could. He set fire to their crops and killed them in battles. One night, the Philistines locked Samson inside the city of Gaza.

They thought he wouldn't be able to escape and they could kill him. But Samson lifted the city gates off the gate posts and carried them away.

Samson fell in love with a beautiful Philistine girl called Delilah. The Philistines promised her a huge sum of money if she could find out why Samson was so strong. Delilah asked Samson to tell her the secret but he teased her with silly stories that weren't true.

"If you really loved me, you'd tell me the truth," she said, and asked him the question again and again. At last, Samson gave in. "My hair has never been cut," he said. "This shows I belong to God. He makes me strong."

That night, Delilah waited until Samson was fast asleep. Then she quietly called one of the Philistines who crept in

and cut off all Samson's hair. When Samson woke up, he was no stronger than any other man.

The Philistines easily captured Samson, they blinded him and tied him up with chains. Then they marched him to the city of Gaza. There they put him in prison and made him work a mill to grind grain into flour. Slowly his hair began to grow again but the Philistines didn't notice it.

One day, the Philistines held a great feast in their temple in praise of their god, Dagon. They told the people that Dagon had helped them to capture Samson. They brought Samson out of his prison so they could laugh at this huge but helpless man. They chained him between two tall pillars which held up the roof of the temple.

Samson was blind but he could feel the pillars. He asked God to give him back his strength. Then he put his huge hands against the pillars and pushed with all his might. He pushed the two pillars over, and the whole temple crashed down. Samson, all the Philistine rulers and thousands of people were killed. This was Samson's greatest show of strength. He had rescued the Israelites from their hated rulers, the Philistines.

Ruth and Naomi

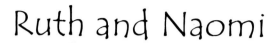

Naomi grew up with her family in the town of Bethlehem but for a long time she had lived far away in Moab. Her husband and two sons had died and she shared a house with her two daughters-in-law, Orpah and Ruth. Now that she was old, Naomi longed to return to Bethlehem and her own people.

"Let us come with you," said Orpah and Ruth, and together the three women started the long journey. On the way, Naomi said, "You should stay in your own country and find new husbands." But the two girls didn't want to leave her. At last, Orpah agreed to stay in Moab but Ruth begged Naomi, "Don't make me leave you. I will go anywhere with you." So Orpah went back to Moab, and Naomi and Ruth went on to Bethlehem.

To get food, Ruth went to the fields every morning and picked up the barley the harvester had left. She ground it into flour to make bread. She didn't know the fields belonged to Naomi's rich relation, Boaz.

Boaz saw Ruth in the fields and asked who she was. When he heard how kind she had been to Naomi, he told her she would be safe in his fields and she could drink all the water she wanted from his servants' water jars.

That evening, Ruth told Naomi about Boaz. Naomi was very pleased for she knew Boaz was a good, kind man. She knew, too, that Boaz slept near his barley harvest so that it wouldn't be stolen. "Go in quietly when Boaz is asleep and lie down near his feet," Naomi said to Ruth.

When Ruth crept in, Boaz heard her. "Who's there?" he asked. "It's Ruth. I've come for your protection," she said. "There is a man who should look after you and marry you," said Boaz. "I'll talk to him tomorrow."

The next day, the man told Boaz he already had a wife. So Boaz married Ruth and, later, they had a son. Naomi was delighted, and was very happy that God had given her a grandson.

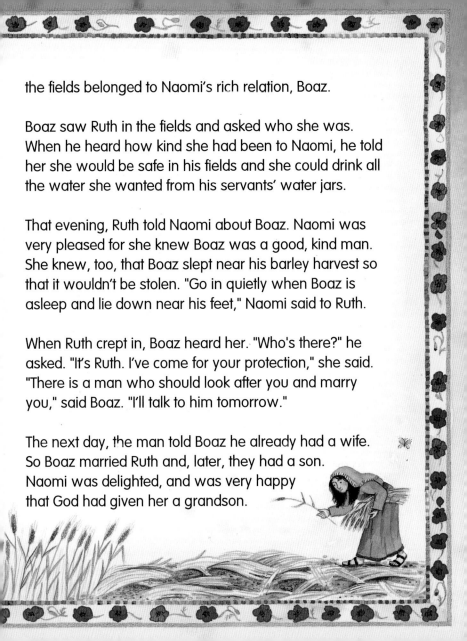

David and Goliath

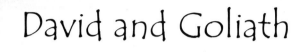

Ruth's great grandson, David, worked on his father's farm. Although he was only a young boy, he looked after his father's sheep out on the hills. He was brave and fought off the wild animals which tried to steal the sheep and lambs, even the fierce lions and bears. He led the flock over the hills to find the best grass for them. And while he watched them, he became very good at firing stones with his sling and playing his little harp.

One day, David's father asked him to take food to his three brothers who were soldiers in King Saul's army. For years King Saul had been fighting the Philistines. Now King Saul's army was camped on one side of a valley. On the other side, was the Philistine army. The two armies watched each other, not daring to attack.

One Philistine soldier was a giant of a man, called Goliath. He was tremendously strong and wore a great helmet and breastplate. He carried a huge shield and a heavy spear.

Every day, he shouted across the valley to King Saul's army, "Send one of your men to fight me. Whoever wins the fight, wins the battle for his whole army."

King Saul's army listened to Goliath's challenge but all the men were too scared to go. When David reached the army camp, he heard Goliath shouting. He said to King Saul, "I'll go and fight."

"You're only a boy. That man is a trained soldier," said King Saul.

"I'm not afraid," said David. "When I was looking after my father's sheep, I killed bears and lions with God's help. God will look after me now because Goliath wants to kill God's people."

"You may go," said King Saul, "but you must wear my fighting clothes and take my sword." David put them on but they were much too big and heavy for him. He took them off again. He picked up his shepherd's stick and chose five small stones from a stream for his sling. Then he strode down the valley to fight Goliath.

When Goliath saw David coming, he made fun of him and shouted, "Come here, boy, and I will kill you."

David walked on. "You have a sword and a spear but I have God to help me," he said. Then he put one of the little stones in his sling, swung the sling around his head, faster and faster, and let it go.

The stone shot out of the sling, straight at Goliath. It hit the giant right in the middle of his forehead. Goliath fell down on the ground. The stone had killed him. David ran up to Goliath and saw that he was dead.

When the Philistine army saw their warrior lying on the ground, they all ran away as fast as they could. King Saul's army chased them, right up to the gates of their city. The battle was over. With God's help, David had won it for them. David grew up to be a great man. He was rich with a huge family and he even became the King.

King Solomon

Solomon, the son of David, was the King of Israel. He lived in the great city of Jerusalem. One night, God came to him and asked, "What would you like me to give you?"

"I'm very young to be a ruler and have a lot to learn. I would like you to make me wise so that I can rule justly and well," said Solomon.

God was very pleased with this answer. "You could have asked to be very rich, very famous and for the death of all your enemies," said God. "But as you have asked for wisdom, I will make you the wisest man in the whole world. I will also make you very rich and famous, and you will live to be very old."

Soon King Solomon became famous for his wise judgements and people came to listen to the many wise things he said.

One day, two women came to his court to ask for his help.

The first woman said, "This woman and I live in the same house. A few days ago, we both gave birth to babies. This woman's baby died, but she stole my baby and now says that it is hers."

"No, your baby died," screamed the second woman. "This baby is mine. I can tell it is my child."

"Bring me my sword," King Solomon ordered one of his guards. When the man brought it, King Solomon said, "Now, cut the baby in half and give one half to each of these women."

One of the women shouted, "Yes, kill the baby and then neither of us can have it." But the other woman cried, "My Lord, please do not kill the child. Give it to this woman and let it live."

King Solomon knew then that this was really the mother and gave her the baby.

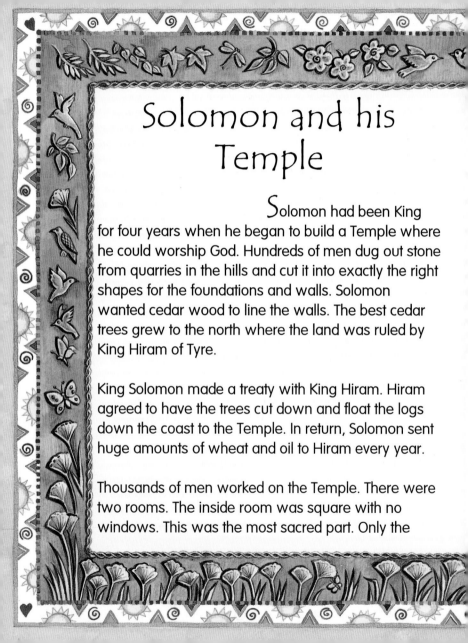

Solomon and his Temple

Solomon had been King for four years when he began to build a Temple where he could worship God. Hundreds of men dug out stone from quarries in the hills and cut it into exactly the right shapes for the foundations and walls. Solomon wanted cedar wood to line the walls. The best cedar trees grew to the north where the land was ruled by King Hiram of Tyre.

King Solomon made a treaty with King Hiram. Hiram agreed to have the trees cut down and float the logs down the coast to the Temple. In return, Solomon sent huge amounts of wheat and oil to Hiram every year.

Thousands of men worked on the Temple. There were two rooms. The inside room was square with no windows. This was the most sacred part. Only the

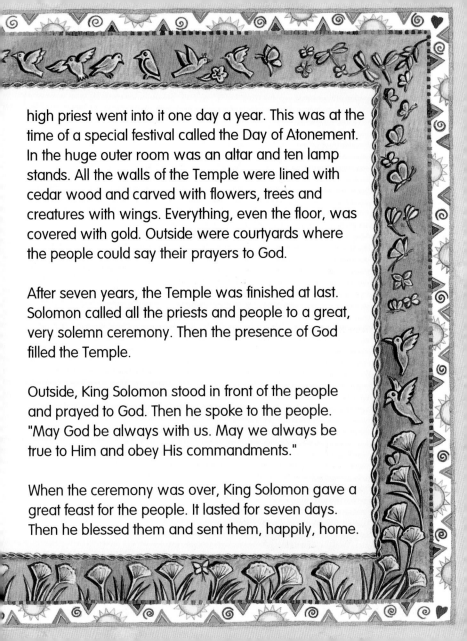

high priest went into it one day a year. This was at the time of a special festival called the Day of Atonement. In the huge outer room was an altar and ten lamp stands. All the walls of the Temple were lined with cedar wood and carved with flowers, trees and creatures with wings. Everything, even the floor, was covered with gold. Outside were courtyards where the people could say their prayers to God.

After seven years, the Temple was finished at last. Solomon called all the priests and people to a great, very solemn ceremony. Then the presence of God filled the Temple.

Outside, King Solomon stood in front of the people and prayed to God. Then he spoke to the people. "May God be always with us. May we always be true to Him and obey His commandments."

When the ceremony was over, King Solomon gave a great feast for the people. It lasted for seven days. Then he blessed them and sent them, happily, home.

Elijah

Elijah lived in Israel and loved and obeyed God. The new King of Israel had built a huge temple to a false god, called Baal, and his Queen was wicked and cruel. Many of the people followed their King and forgot about God. Elijah warned them that there would be no rain for many years and they would starve.

God said to Elijah, "Go to the Kerith valley and live there in safety. You can drink water from the stream and ravens will bring you food."

Elijah did as God told him and every morning and evening the ravens brought him bread and meat, and he drank water from the stream.

But, after a while,
the stream dried up
because there was no
rain. Then God told him to go
to the city of Sidon where a
woman would give him food.

There Elijah met a woman picking up a few
sticks for her fire. "Please give me a drink
of water and some bread," said Elijah.
"I have no food," said the
woman. "All I have is a
little flour and a few
drops of olive oil. I'm
going to bake one
loaf over a fire of

these sticks. When we have eaten the loaf, my son and I will starve to death."

"Go home," said Elijah, "and bake a small loaf for me and one for you and your son. From now on, you'll find that your flour and oil for bread will never run out."

The woman did what Elijah told her and found that every day she always had just enough flour and oil to make bread. But, one day, the woman's son became very ill and died. The woman was heartbroken. "Why have you killed my son?" she asked Elijah. "Is it to punish me for the wrong things I've done in my life?"

"Give the boy to me," said Elijah. He carried the boy upstairs and laid him on his bed. There he prayed three times to God, "Please bring this boy back to life."

God answered Elijah's prayer. The boy sat up, alive and well. Elijah picked him up and carried him down to his mother. "Look," he said, "your son is alive." The woman was overjoyed. "I know now that you are a man of God and what you say is true," she said.

Elisha and Naaman

Naaman was the commander of the Syrian army. He was a brave soldier and a rich man with a big house and lots of servants, but he had a horrible skin disease, called leprosy.

Naaman's wife had a new slave. She was a young girl who had been captured by the Syrians during a raid on Israel. She said to Naaman's wife, "If lord Naaman could go to the prophet Elisha in Israel, I know he would be cured of his disease."

When Naaman was told what the slave had said, he went to the King of Syria. The King gave Naaman leave to go to Israel and gave him a letter for the King of Israel. Naaman rode off in his chariot with his servants, taking gifts of silver and gold, and clothes for Elisha. When he reached Elisha's house, a servant came to the door.

"My master says that you must go to the Jordan and

wash in the river seven times," said the servant. "Then you will be cured."

Naaman was very angry. "Why won't Elisha come out to see me?" he shouted. "I thought he'd call on his God and I'd be cured. And why must I wash in the Jordan? There are lots of much better rivers in Syria."

He started to drive away in his chariot but one of his servants stopped him. "My master," said the servant, "if Elisha had asked you to do something difficult, you would have done it. As he only says you should wash in the Jordan, shouldn't you try it?"

Namaan realized that the servant was right. He went to the Jordan and washed in it seven times. When he walked out of the river, his skin was clear and smooth. He was cured of the disease.

Delighted, he rushed back to Elisha to thank him. "I know now," said Naaman, "that there is only one true God." He tried to give Elisha all the gifts he had brought from Syria but Elisha wouldn't take them. He blessed Naaman and sent him home.

Daniel and the Lions

Daniel was only a boy when Jerusalem was captured by the Babylonians. He was taken, with other people, to the magnificent city of Babylon. There he and other boys were given plenty of tasty food, a good schooling, and were taken care of. But Daniel never forgot he came from Israel, and he prayed to God three times every day.

Daniel grew up strong and wise. When King Darius ruled Babylon, he made Daniel one of the three rulers of the whole kingdom. The other two rulers were jealous of Daniel and plotted to get rid of him. But they couldn't find that Daniel had done anything wrong.

In the end, they went to King Darius. "Make a new law, O King," they said. "For thirty days everyone must pray only to you. If anyone prays to any god, they shall be fed to the lions." The King made the law.

Daniel heard about the law but three times every day he still knelt at his window to say his prayers to God.

The two rulers watched and then went off to report him to the King.

The King was very upset. He liked and trusted Daniel but he couldn't save him from the law. He ordered Daniel to be put into the lion pit. As Daniel walked down into it, and the entrance was closed up with a huge stone, the King said "May your God save you."

King Darius went back to his palace. That night, he was so upset, he couldn't eat any supper. He sent his servants away and couldn't sleep. Early the next morning, he went to the lion pit. "Did your God save you?" he shouted to Daniel. "I am here," answered Daniel. "God kept the lions' mouths shut. He knows I've done nothing wrong."

The King was delighted that Daniel was safe. He ordered him to be taken out of the pit. Then he ordered the two rulers to be put into the pit with the lions.

The King made a new law. He ordered that everyone in his kingdom should respect Daniel's God, the God who had saved Daniel from the lions.

Brave Esther

King Xerxes was rich and powerful and ruled the huge Persian empire. After he had been king for three years, he gave a magnificent feast which lasted for seven days. Thousands of guests were served the most delicious food and drank the best wines out of golden cups.

One night, he said to one of his servants, "Bring Queen Vashti here to me." He wanted everyone to see how beautiful his queen was. But Queen Vashti was holding her own feast and sent a message saying that she wouldn't come. King Xerxes was furious with her. He ordered her out of his palace and announced that she was no longer his wife.

King Xerxes wanted a new queen. He sent his servants all over his kingdom to find the most beautiful girls so that he could choose one for his new wife.

A man called Mordecai worked in King Xerxes' palace. He was from Jerusalem. He had a young cousin, called

Esther, whom he had brought up as his own daughter because her father and mother were dead. She was a beautiful girl who was always sweet-tempered and kind.

When King Xerxes looked at the girls brought from all over his kingdom, he chose Esther to be his new wife. Soon she was crowned Queen Esther. But Mordecai warned her many times never to tell anyone she was a Hebrew and not a Persian girl.

One day, Mordecai heard two men whispering together. They were plotting to kill King Xerxes. "You must warn your husband," Mordecai said to Esther and told her who these men were. Esther told the King, who had the two men put to death. He was very pleased that Esther and Mordecai were loyal to him.

The King's chief of staff was a proud and cruel man called Haman. Everyone had to bow to him but Mordecai would not bow. "I am a Jew. My people and I bow only to God," he said. Haman was very angry. He told the King that some people were making trouble in his kingdom. The King said he should deal with them in any way he liked. Haman ordered that Mordecai and all the Jewish people be killed on a certain day. No one knew that Queen Esther was also a Jew.

When Esther heard the news, she was very upset. Mordecai said to her, "You must go to the King and beg him to save the lives of your people."

"I can't do that," Esther replied. "I always have to wait for the King to send for me. If I go to him, he may be angry and have me killed."

"God may have made you the Queen so that you can save us," said Mordecai.

Esther was terrified but she went to the King. Haman was there with him. She invited both of them to dinner the next day. The King was very pleased and Haman felt very proud to be dining with the King and Queen. But then he thought of Mordecai and how the Jew would not bow to him. Very angry, he ordered that Mordecai should be hung the next morning.

That night King Xerxes could not sleep. Reading through the palace records, he came across Mordecai's name and remembered that Mordecai had saved his life. "I must reward him," said King Xerxes. So, instead of being hanged in the morning, Mordecai was rewarded by the King who ordered he should be given rich clothes and a fine horse.

When King Xerxes and Haman went to dine with Esther the next day, Esther begged the King for a kindness. The King looked at his beautiful wife. "You may have anything you wish for. You only have to ask," he said.

"I and all my people are to be killed," Esther said. "Please will you save us?" The King was horrified. "Who dared to give the order for this?" he demanded. "It was Haman," said Esther.

Haman knelt in front of Esther and begged her to save him, but King Xerxes ordered him to be hanged. Then the King ordered that all the Jewish people in his kingdom were not to be killed, but were to be treated well and with respect. Esther had saved her people from death.

Jonah and the Whale

Jonah was a good man who usually did what God told him. But one day, God told Jonah to go to the city of Nineveh. He was to tell the people there that God had seen that they were very bad and would punish them.

Jonah didn't want to go. Instead, he ran away to the port at Joppa and found a ship that was going to Tarshish, a very long way from Nineveh. He thought God wouldn't be able to see him there. He paid his fare and went on board the ship.

As soon as it sailed off across the sea, there was a huge storm. It had been sent by God. The sailors were terrified and threw everything overboard to make the ship lighter because it was in danger of sinking. The captain told them to pray to their gods to save them.

All through the storm, Jonah lay fast asleep in the bottom of the ship. The captain went to Jonah and shook him to wake him up. "You must pray too," he shouted.

"I can't pray to God," Jonah shouted back. "I'm running away from Him."

The sailors thought Jonah had brought the storm and they would all die. They begged him to tell them how to make the water calm. "You must throw me in the sea," said Jonah. But the captain told the sailors, "I can't kill this man."

"You must," said Jonah. "You'll die unless you throw me overboard. Then the storm will stop." The storm grew worse and worse and, at last, the captain agreed.

The sailors threw Jonah into the sea and, at once, the storm was over. The sailors thanked Jonah's God for saving their lives.

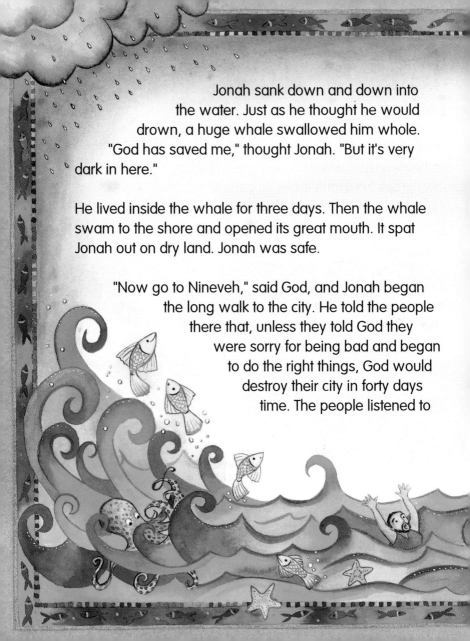

Jonah sank down and down into the water. Just as he thought he would drown, a huge whale swallowed him whole. "God has saved me," thought Jonah. "But it's very dark in here."

He lived inside the whale for three days. Then the whale swam to the shore and opened its great mouth. It spat Jonah out on dry land. Jonah was safe.

"Now go to Nineveh," said God, and Jonah began the long walk to the city. He told the people there that, unless they told God they were sorry for being bad and began to do the right things, God would destroy their city in forty days time. The people listened to

Jonah and the King ordered them to be sorry for their badness and pray to God.

Jonah sat outside the city and waited for it to be destroyed. He was very hot and very cross. He wanted God to destroy Nineveh. But God saw that the people had turned to Him and He saved the city.

"Jonah, I love all the people in Nineveh," said God, "and I am everywhere. You can't run away from me." And Jonah knew that this was true.

The New
Testament

Contents

Mary and the Angel

Mary lived in Nazareth, a village in the hills of Galilee. She was engaged to be married to Joseph, a carpenter who lived in the village.

One day, God sent an angel called Gabriel to Mary. "Don't be frightened," he said. "God has sent me to tell you that you will have a son and you must call him Jesus. He will be a great King and his kingdom will last forever."

Mary was very puzzled. "I don't understand," she said to Gabriel. "How can I have a son? I'm not married yet."

"It will be the work of God, who can do anything," said Gabriel. "Your son will be holy and will be the Son of God."

Mary bowed her head. "I am God's servant. I'll do what He wants," she said. When she looked up, Gabriel had gone.

Joseph was a kind man but when he heard

that Mary was expecting a baby, he thought it was not right for him to marry her.

That night, he had a dream. In it an angel told him that he should marry Mary and that her son was the Son of God. He would be called Jesus and he would save people from God's punishment for the bad things they had done.

Next day, Joseph remembered what the angel had told him. He made arrangements for the wedding and soon they were married. Joseph vowed to take care of Mary and her baby son.

The Birth of Jesus

Mary and Joseph lived happily together and looked forward to the birth of the baby Mary was expecting. A few months later, the Roman Emperor Augustus, who ruled the whole country, made a new law. Everyone must go to the town their family came from to register so they could be taxed. Joseph's family had come from Bethlehem, so he had to go back there.

He started on the long journey with Mary, who was expecting her baby quite soon. They loaded up their donkey with warm clothes, food, water, and things for the baby.

It was late when they reached Bethlehem and Mary was very tired. The small town was crowded and noisy with all the people who had come to register. Joseph tried to find a room to stay in for the night, but everywhere was already full up. He trudged through the cold, dark streets, leading the donkey Mary rode on.

He knocked on the door of the last inn but it was already

full, not one room left. There was a stable nearby though, which was clean and empty.

Joseph led the donkey to the stable. He helped Mary down. Then he made a soft bed of straw for her on the floor and covered it with his cloak. Mary ate some food and then lay down, thankful that she could rest at last.

That night, Mary's baby son was born. She washed him and wrapped him in the clothes she had brought with her. Joseph filled a manger with soft, clean hay to make a bed for the baby and Mary laid him gently in it. She called her new baby Jesus, as the angel had told her to, and he was the Son of God.

Out on the hills near Bethlehem, some shepherds lay around their camp fire, guarding their flocks of sheep during the night. Suddenly, they saw a brilliant light in the dark sky and an angel stood in front of them. They were very scared.

"Don't be frightened," said the angel. "I have wonderful news for you, and for all people. Tonight the Son of God was born in a stable in Bethlehem."

As the shepherds stared at the angel, more angels appeared in the sky, singing praises to God. "Glory to God in the highest and peace on earth to all people who love him," they sang. Then the light faded and the angels were gone. The night was dark again.

The shepherds were very excited. "We must go to Bethlehem and look for this child," said one shepherd. The others agreed. They gathered up their things and ran as quickly as they could down the dark hills to the little town.

They soon found the stable and, knocking on the door, crept

quietly in. They
looked at the baby
lying in the manger
and knelt down in front of him.
They told Mary and Joseph what the
angel had said to them.

After a while, the shepherds got up and left
the stable. They strode through the streets of
Bethlehem, telling everyone they met the good
news that the Son of God had been born that
night. Soon the whole town knew about the
birth of Jesus.

Singing praises to God, the shepherds
walked very happily back to their
sheep on the dark hills outside
Bethlehem.

In the quiet stable, Mary looked at her baby son and thought about the shepherds and what the angel had told them. She wondered about it all.

The Wise Men

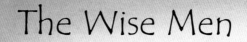

In a country far from Bethlehem lived some Wise Men who studied the stars. One night they saw a new star which was much brighter than all the rest. They knew it must mean something special had happened. After a lot of study, they decided that it meant a new ruler had been born and that they must go to find him.

They began their long journey, taking presents for this new ruler. They followed the star which moved across the night sky ahead of them. At last they arrived in the great city of Jerusalem.

"Tell us where we can find this baby," they said. "We have seen his star in the sky and know he is born to be the King of the Jews."

When King Herod heard that three strangers were trying to find the baby, he was angry and frightened. The Roman rulers of the country had made Herod the King of the Jews. He asked his priests and wise men what it meant. They studied the old records, and told King Herod that, many years ago, it had been forecast that the King of the Jews would be born in Bethlehem.

Herod asked for a secret meeting with the Wise Men. When they came, he told them to go to Bethlehem. "When you find this child, let me know so that I can worship him too," he said. The Wise Men agreed and started at once along the road to Bethlehem. The star still moved ahead of them and then seemed to stop over the town. The Wise Men knew that they'd come to the right place.

They soon found out where Mary and Joseph were. When they saw baby Jesus, the Wise Men knelt down in front of him and gave Mary the presents they had brought with them. The presents were gold, and sweet-smelling frankincense, and a special ointment called myrrh. Then the Wise Men went quietly away.

On their way back to King Herod in Jerusalem, they camped outside Bethlehem. That night, they had a dream. In it, an angel warned them that King Herod planned to kill Jesus. In the morning, they loaded their camels and went, not to Jerusalem, but by a different road back to their own country.

Joseph also had a dream. An angel warned him that Jesus was in danger and he must take Mary and the

baby to Egypt where they would be safe. Joseph woke Mary, and quickly packed up their things. Carrying baby Jesus, they started on their long journey to Egypt while it was still dark.

When King Herod realized he'd been tricked by the Wise Men, he was furious. He was afraid that this new King of the Jews would seize his throne. He ordered his soldiers to march to Bethlehem and kill all the boys under two years old. The people had always hated this cruel king and now they hated him even more.

Mary and Joseph lived safely with Jesus in Egypt. Then Joseph had another dream. An angel told him that King Herod was dead and he should take Mary and Jesus back to Nazareth. After another very long journey, they settled down in their own home.

Jesus in the Temple

Jesus grew up in Nazareth, cared for by Mary and Joseph. He went to school and learned the laws God had given to the Jews. Every year, Mary and Joseph went to Jerusalem to celebrate the Feast of the Passover. This festival reminded them that God had freed his people from slavery in Egypt all those years ago.

When Jesus was twelve years old, he went to Jerusalem with his parents. The journey took four days and when they arrived the great city was crowded with visitors.

When the festival was over, Mary and Joseph joined the other families going back to Nazareth. They thought Jesus was in the crowd with the other boys. It wasn't until they stopped in the evening to camp for the night and have a meal that they realized that Jesus was missing. They looked everywhere for him and asked everyone if they had seen him, but they couldn't find him.

Very worried, Mary and Joseph hurried back to Jerusalem. For three days, they searched the city for Jesus. At last, they found him in the Temple. He was sitting with the Temple teachers, listening to them and asking questions. The teachers were amazed that Jesus, who was only twelve, understood so much of what they told him, and were astonished by the questions he asked. Mary and Joseph were very surprised to find him there.

"Why did you do this to us?" Mary asked Jesus. "We've been searching everywhere for you. We were so worried about you. We thought we'd never find you."

"I'm sorry I have caused so much trouble," said Jesus. "But didn't you know you would find me in my Father's house?"

Mary and Joseph didn't understand what Jesus meant. They took him home to Nazareth where he grew up into a wise and strong young man who loved and obeyed his parents and God.

Jesus is Baptized

Jesus stayed in Nazareth with Mary and Joseph until he was about thirty years old. Then he went to Galilee where John, a cousin of his, was telling the people about God and how they should do what He says. Crowds of people came to hear him. When they asked John what they should do, he told them to share their food with hungry people and give their spare clothes to those who needed them.

John baptized the people who were sorry for the bad things they had done. He used water in the Jordan river. This meant they were sorry for their bad

lives and could start again by leading good lives.

"I baptize you with water," John told them, "but one is coming who is much greater than I. I'm not worthy to undo his sandals. He will baptize you with the Holy Spirit."

Jesus went to John and asked John to baptize him. But John said, "It's not right for me to baptize you. You should baptize me."

"Let us do what God wants," said Jesus and, saying a prayer, he walked into the river. John poured water over Jesus to show that he had been washed clean. Then, just as Jesus stepped out of the river, Heaven opened and a white dove hovered over his head. And he heard the voice of God say to him, "You are my dear Son. I am very pleased with you."

Jesus and his Disciples

Jesus lived in Capernaum, a town near Lake Galilee. There he talked to people about God, and healed the ones who were ill. News of his teaching spread quickly and, everywhere he went, crowds of people came to listen to him.

One day, Jesus was walking along the shore of the lake. As usual, people crowded around him. There was a boat pulled up on the shore, owned by a fisherman called Peter and his brother Andrew. Jesus stepped into it. "Row a little way out on the lake so I can speak to the people," said Jesus. The two men did as Jesus asked.

Later, Jesus told Peter and Andrew to row farther away from the shore and put out their fishing nets. "We have fished all night and caught nothing," said Peter. But they did as Jesus told them. When they began to pull in the nets, they were so full of fish, the nets were almost breaking. Peter and Andrew shouted across to two other fishermen, James and John, to come to help. Together, they filled both boats with fish.

92

When the four men
saw how many fish
they'd caught, they were
very frightened and knelt in front
of Jesus. "Don't be afraid," said Jesus.
"Come with me and I will make you fishermen of people."

Peter and Andrew, James and John rowed back to the
shore and unloaded the fish. Then they left their boats and
went with Jesus on his journeys.

One day, Jesus saw a rich man called Matthew. He
worked for the Romans, collecting taxes. The Jewish
people hated the Romans who ruled them, and hated their
tax collectors even more. Jesus said to Matthew, "Come
with me." Without saying a word, Matthew stood up and
followed Jesus and the other disciples.

Matthew gave a feast in his house for Jesus. Some religious people saw Jesus there. They asked Jesus' friends why such a good man sat down at a table with so many bad people. Jesus heard them. "Healthy people don't need a doctor," he said. "It's the sick who need help. I have come to ask the bad people to change their ways. The good people don't need me."

One evening Jesus walked high up a mountain and stayed there all night, praying to God. The next day, he chose the rest of his disciples. They were Philip and Bartholomew, Thomas, another James, Simon, Judas and Judas Iscariot. With Peter, Andrew, James, John and Matthew, these twelve men were Jesus' special friends and followers. They went everywhere with him, listened to his teachings and watched the wonderful things he did. He told them what God had sent him to do.

Jesus and the Paralysed Man

News that Jesus was teaching people about God and making those who were ill well again spread very quickly. Wherever he went with his twelve disciples, crowds of people came from all over the country, and from the city of Jerusalem, to listen to him and to be healed of all kinds of diseases.

One day, Jesus was sitting in a house that was so packed with people, there was no room for anyone to move in or out. Four friends of a very ill man carried him on a stretcher to the house. The man was paralysed and couldn't move at all.

When the four friends saw they couldn't get into the house by the door, they lifted the stretcher up to the flat roof. Then they made a hole in the roof and lowered the stretcher and the sick man down into the room where Jesus was sitting.

Jesus looked at the four friends and saw the faith they had in him. Then he said to the sick man, "My son," he said, "your sins are forgiven."

The Jewish leaders who heard Jesus say this whispered angrily to each other. Jesus had no right to forgive sins, they said; only God could do that.

Jesus knew what they were saying. "Is it easier," he asked them, "to forgive a man for the bad things he has done or to make him walk again? To show you that I have the power to forgive sins. . ." Jesus stopped and turned to the man on the stretcher. "Get up, pick up your stretcher and go home," he said.

Without saying a word, the man at once stood up and, taking the stretcher with him, walked out of the house. He went home, saying a prayer of thanks to God.

The people in the house were very excited and a little frightened. They talked to each other and praised God. They had never seen anything like this before.

The Sermon on the Mountain

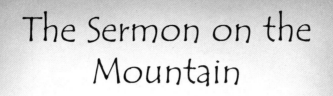

Wherever Jesus went with his disciples, crowds of people came to listen to him. On the Sabbath, he taught them in the synagogues, but most of the time he talked to them out of doors, as the weather was often hot and dry.

One day, he walked up a mountain. The people sat down so they could see and hear him. Jesus told them that those people who were really hungry to know God would be satisfied. He told them they should be content and not worry about food or clothing. "Look at the birds," he said. "They don't grow

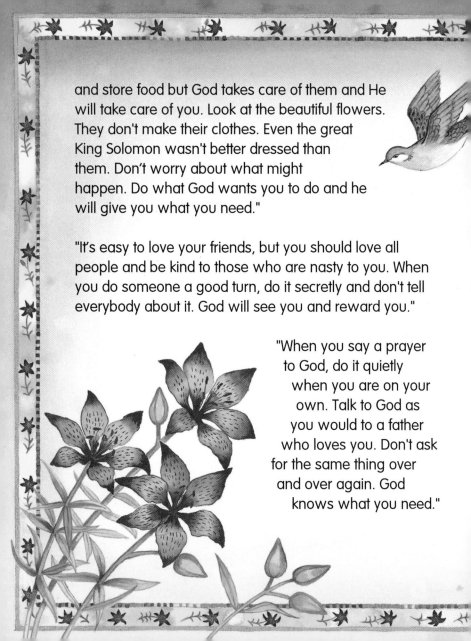

and store food but God takes care of them and He will take care of you. Look at the beautiful flowers. They don't make their clothes. Even the great King Solomon wasn't better dressed than them. Don't worry about what might happen. Do what God wants you to do and he will give you what you need."

"It's easy to love your friends, but you should love all people and be kind to those who are nasty to you. When you do someone a good turn, do it secretly and don't tell everybody about it. God will see you and reward you."

"When you say a prayer to God, do it quietly when you are on your own. Talk to God as you would to a father who loves you. Don't ask for the same thing over and over again. God knows what you need."

"Say this prayer when you speak to God:
    Our Father who is in Heaven
    Holy is your name,
    May your Kingdom come,
    May your will be done on earth as it is in Heaven.
    Give us our food each day,
    Forgive us the wrongs we have done,
    As we forgive the wrongs others have done to us.
    Do not let us be tempted to do wrong.
    But save us from evil."

"Anyone who listens to me," said Jesus, "and does what I say is like a man who builds a house on solid rock. When it rains and the wind blows and the floods come, his house will stand strong and firm. But anyone who hears me and does not do what I say is like a man who builds his house on the sand. When it rains, the wind blows and the floods come, his house will be washed away because it was built only on soft sand."

Jesus Calms the Storm

One evening, when Jesus was tired after talking to people all day and making the sick ones well again, he asked some of his disciples to take him across Lake Galilee. There was just a gentle breeze blowing when they pushed the boat down the beach and floated it on the lake. The disciples hoisted the sail and the boat skimmed away across the smooth water.

Jesus lay down in the
bottom of the boat and was
soon fast asleep.

Suddenly the wind started blowing
stronger and stronger until there was a
great storm. The waves grew bigger and bigger
and splashed over the side of the boat. The
disciples were very scared. Some of them were
fishermen and knew how dangerous storms on the
lake could be. They thought the boat would fill with
water and sink. Although the wind was so noisy and the
waves so rough, Jesus just slept on.

At last, one of the disciples could bear it no longer. He shook Jesus and woke him up.

"Master, please save us," he shouted. "Can't you see that we're all going to drown?"

Jesus woke up and looked at the storm for a moment. Then he stood up, raised his arm and said, "Hush, be still." At once, the wind died away and the waves became calm.

"Why were you afraid?" Jesus asked the disciples. "Don't you believe I will take care of you?"

The disciples didn't know what to say. They whispered to each other. "Who is this man that even the wind and the waves do as he tells them?"

The boat sailed on and Jesus and his disciples safely reached the far shore of the lake.

The Good Shepherd

Jesus often told people stories so that they could understand more easily what he was trying to teach them. The stories were about the things they saw every day and some of the work they did. He said to the men, women and children who came to hear him, "If you have ears, listen to what I say."

One day, he began a new story. "If a shepherd has a hundred sheep to look after and one of them wanders off and gets lost, what does the shepherd do?" he asked the people. "He leaves the ninety-nine sheep," Jesus went on, "where he knows they are safe from hungry wolves and goes off in search of the one missing sheep."

"The shepherd searches everywhere for that one sheep, listening all the time to hear it bleating. However long it takes, he doesn't give up until he finds it. Then he picks up the sheep, puts it on his shoulders and carries it home, delighted that it is safely back with the rest of the flock."

"Then he calls his family and friends to come and celebrate with him that he has found his one lost sheep."

"There is joy in Heaven," said Jesus, "when someone who has disobeyed God is sorry for the bad things he or she has done and comes back to do as God wants them to do."

"I am like that good shepherd. I look after my people as if they were my sheep. I never run away and leave them when wolves try to kill them. The sheep know my voice and follow me. I lead them and protect them. I am ready to die for them," said Jesus.

Jairus's Daughter

When Jesus was walking through a town one day, a ruler of the synagogue, called Jairus, ran up to him. He knelt in front of Jesus. "My little daughter is very ill; I think she is dying. Please come to my house and put your hands on her so she may get better," he begged.

As Jesus started to go with Jairus, a woman pushed through the crowd following them to get near to Jesus. She had been ill for twelve years and none of the doctors had been able to help her; she only got worse.

She had heard of Jesus. She thought, "If I could only touch his clothes, I know I will be well at last." When she was close, she put out her hand and touched him. At once, she was completely cured. Jesus looked at the people crowding around him. "Who touched me?" he asked, knowing that someone had been healed.

The woman was very frightened. She knelt in front of Jesus and told him she had touched him. Jesus looked

 at her and smiled. "Your faith has made you well," he said. "Go in peace."

Jesus walked on to Jairus's house but, before he got there, people came out weeping. "It is too late," they cried to Jairus. "Your little daughter is dead. Don't ask Jesus to come."

"She is not dead. She is asleep," said Jesus, and he went on to the house, with three disciples, Peter, James and John. Jesus made everyone leave the house, except the mother and father of the little girl. Then he gently held the girl's hand and said, "Little girl, get up."

At once, the girl opened her eyes and got up off her bed. The girl's mother and father were astonished and thrilled to see their daughter alive and well. "Now give her something to eat," said Jesus, "but don't tell anyone about this." And he and his three disciples walked quietly out of the house.

Loaves and Fishes

One day, Jesus was feeling tired and wanted to go to a quiet place to have a little time by himself. He and his disciples sailed across Lake Galilee to a lonely beach. They landed on the shore, pulled up the boat and walked up a hill to rest. But some people had seen where Jesus went and news that he was there quickly spread. Soon people started to walk from the towns and villages to see and hear him.

The disciples wanted to send the people away but Jesus felt sorry for them. He walked among them, talking to them, answering their questions and making the ill ones well. More and more people came until there were thousands of them.

In the evening, a disciple said to Jesus, "It's time these people went home. Send them away now so they can find food. There's nothing here for them to eat."

Jesus said, "They are hungry, we must feed them first."

"There is nowhere to buy food, and even a huge amount of money wouldn't buy enough to feed all these people," said Philip, one of the disciples.

Andrew, another disciple, said to Jesus, "There is a boy here who has five small loaves and two fishes."

Jesus looked down at the boy. "May I take your food?" Jesus asked him. "Yes, Master," said the boy.

"Tell the people to sit down in groups," Jesus said to the disciples. The disciples walked through the crowd asking everyone to sit down on the grass. There were about five thousand men, women and children.

Jesus held up the boy's five small loaves and two little fishes, and said a prayer to God. Then he broke up the bread and fishes and handed them to the disciples to give to the people. The more food the disciples gave out, the more there was. They were very surprised and very puzzled.

Everybody began to eat and they all had as much as they wanted. When the meal was over, the people got up and went home in the late evening.

"Collect all the leftover food," Jesus said to the disciples. They walked over the hillside, picking up the food. When they'd finished, they'd filled twelve baskets with bits of bread and fish.

The Good Samaritan

When Jesus was teaching the people about God, a clever lawyer stood up and asked him, "I know I should be kind to other people, but who does that mean?"

Jesus told him this story. "A Jew who lived in Jerusalem left the city and began the long walk to Jericho. Although the Jew knew it was dangerous to travel alone, because there were robbers on the road, he went on his own."

"When the Jew came to a lonely spot, some robbers rushed out and attacked him. They beat him, knocked him down and kicked him. Then they stole all he had and ran away, leaving him lying on the ground, badly wounded."

"After a while, a priest from the Temple came down the road. He saw the Jew lying in the dust, but dug his heels into his donkey and hurried away."

"Later, a man who worked in the Temple in Jerusalem came up. He looked at the wounded Jew for a moment but didn't stop. He went on quickly away down the road."

"Then a Samaritan trotted up on his donkey. The Samaritans and the Jews had always hated each other. But this Samaritan felt sorry for the Jew. He stopped and got off his donkey. He opened his pack and, kneeling by the man, poured oil on his wounds to ease the pain and gave him wine to drink to make him feel better. Then he bandaged the man with strips of cloth."

"When the Samaritan had done all he could, he lifted the Jew up on his donkey and led it down the road to an inn. There he put the Jew to bed and bought him supper."

"The next morning, the Samaritan paid the innkeeper. 'Look after this man for me,' he said. 'I will pay you any extra money I owe you when I come this way again.'"

"Now," Jesus asked the lawyer, "which of the three men was kind?"

"The Samaritan, of course," replied the lawyer. "That is the answer to your question," said Jesus. "You should be kind to everyone, not just your family and friends, but everyone."

Mary, Martha and Lazarus

When Jesus visited a village called Bethany, near Jerusalem, he stayed with two sisters, Mary and Martha, and their brother Lazarus.

One day, Mary and Martha sent a message to Jesus, telling him that Lazarus was very ill and asking him to come and save their brother's life. They expected Jesus to come at once, but they waited for two days and Jesus still had not come.

"Our friend Lazarus is sleeping. I'll go and wake him up," Jesus said to his twelve disciples. "Won't sleep make him better?" asked the disciples. But Jesus knew that Lazarus was dead.

When Jesus and his disciples reached Bethany at last, Lazarus had been in his tomb for four days. Mary stayed in the house with her weeping friends but Martha ran out to meet Jesus. "Lord, if you had been here, my brother would not have died," she cried.

"He will live again," said Jesus.

"I know he will when God brings all the dead back to life on the last day," said Martha. "Everyone who trusts in me will live for ever, even if they die," Jesus said to her.

Then Mary came out of the house, crying, with the friends and relations who had come to comfort her. Jesus felt very sorry for her and was sad. "Take me to Lazarus," he said. They led him to the tomb which was a cave. In front of it was a big rock. "Move the rock away," said Jesus.

"But Lazarus has been dead for four days. He will smell bad," said Martha. "I told you that if you would trust me, you shall see God's glory," Jesus told her.

Friends of the two sisters rolled away the rock in front of the tomb. Jesus said a prayer to God and then shouted, "Lazarus, come out."

Lazarus walked out of the tomb, wearing the clothes he had been buried in, but alive and well.

The Prodigal Son

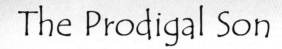

Jesus was talking to a crowd of people when some of the religious people muttered, "Why does this man talk and eat with bad people?" Jesus heard them and told them, "When only one bad person is sorry for what he has done and wants to please God, there is joy in Heaven." And he told them this story.

"A rich farmer had two sons. One day, the younger son said, 'Father, one day half of everything you have will be mine. Give it to me now.' The father was very unhappy but he did as his son demanded and gave him a lot of his money."

"A few days later, the son rode away to a city, taking the money with him. He bought rich clothes and a big house with lots of servants, and soon made many new friends. Every evening, he gave great feasts for his friends, with delicious food and good wine."

"He thought he was having a wonderful time. But soon he had spent all his money. His new friends left him, his house and servants were taken away from him, and he had nothing left, not even his fine clothes."

"He wandered the streets, begging for something to eat. But as there was a shortage of food in the city, no one had any to spare, and he had to go hungry."

"At last he got a job looking after a man's pigs in the fields. Sometimes he was so hungry, he was tempted to eat the pigs' food. One day, as he was watching the pigs, he thought, 'My father's servants always have plenty to eat, while I'm nearly dying of hunger. I'll go home and beg my father to forgive me.'"

"After a long journey, the son reached his home, tired, dirty and wearing rags. When he was still some way from the house, his father saw him. He felt very sorry for his son and ran to meet him. He threw his arms around him and hugged him."

"'Forgive me, father. I've been very foolish,' said the son. 'I don't deserve to be your son any more. Let me be one of your servants.'"

"The father took his son home. He told his servants to bring new clothes and shoes for his son. He was so happy, he ordered a special dinner that night and told everyone they should join in the party."

"Out in the fields, the elder son heard the noise of laughter and music. He walked back to the house and asked one of the servants what it was all about."

"'Your brother has come home and your father is giving him a special dinner, with music and dancing, because he is so pleased to see his son again,' said the servant."

"The elder son was very angry and refused to go into the house. His father went out and asked him to come in."

"'I've worked hard for you all these years but you've never given me anything. You've never given a party for me and my friends,' shouted the son. 'But as soon as your other son comes home, having wasted half your money, you order a great feast for him.'"

"'My son,' said the father, 'you are always with me and everything I have is yours. Please try to understand. I thought your brother was lost or dead. I'm so happy he has come home again, alive and well.'"

Jesus Rides into Jerusalem

Jesus and his twelve disciples walked to the great city of Jerusalem to be there in time for the special festival of the Passover. On the way, they stopped near a small village called Bethany.

Jesus said to two of his disciples, "Go into the village. There you will find a donkey that has never been ridden. Untie it and

bring it here. If anyone asks you why you are taking it, tell him, 'The Lord needs it,' and he will let you have it."

The two disciples did as Jesus told them and soon came back with the donkey. They spread their cloaks over it to make a soft saddle and Jesus got on

the donkey. Then he rode into Jerusalem with his disciples walking at his side.

When the crowds of people walking to the city saw Jesus coming, they were excited. Some spread their cloaks on the road. Others cut down palm leaves to lay in front of him. They cheered and shouted, "Blessed is he who comes in the name of the Lord. Praise be to God."

Jesus and his disciples went into the city and walked through the streets to the Temple. Then they left and went back to the village of Bethany for the night.

The next morning, Jesus went again to the Temple to pray. It was like a crowded market with people buying and selling cows, sheep and doves, and changing money. Jesus was very angry. He stormed through it, overturning the tables and the seats of the sellers and driving them, and the animals and birds out of the Temple.

"God's house is a house of prayer," he shouted, "but you have turned it into a den of robbers."

When all was quiet and peaceful again, he talked to the

crowds of people, teaching them about God and making the ill ones well again.

The Temple rulers heard what Jesus had done and decided they must get rid of him. They didn't dare arrest him in the Temple because they were afraid the people would riot to protect him. They plotted to do it secretly.

Then Judas Iscariot, one of Jesus' disciples, went secretly to the chief priests of the Temple. "What will you give me if I tell you when it would be safe to arrest Jesus?" he asked. They promised to give him thirty silver coins. From then on, Judas Iscariot waited and watched for the right moment to give Jesus away to the Temple priests. It had to be when there were no crowds around to see the arrest.

The Last Supper

A few days before the Feast of the Passover, which reminded the Jews of when God freed them from being slaves in Egypt, Jesus' disciples asked him where they should have the special meal.

"Go to Jerusalem," said Jesus to Peter and John. "There you will meet a man carrying a jar of water. Follow him to his house. We will have our meal there in a room upstairs."

The two men went to Jerusalem and found the house. They made the room ready and that evening Jesus and the other ten disciples came upstairs.

Before the meal began, Jesus picked up a towel and a bowl of water. He knelt in front of each disciple in turn, and washed their feet and dried them with a towel, just like a servant. When he had finished, he said, "You must be ready to serve each other in the same way that I have served you."

Then Jesus sat down again at the table. The disciples watched him quietly. They could see something was wrong. Jesus looked very sad because he knew he wouldn't be with them much longer, but would die soon.

At last, he said, "One of you will betray me." The disciples were horrified. They all looked at each other and wondered who it could be. Then one, who was sitting next to Jesus, asked, "Which one of us is it, Lord?" "It is the one I give this bread to," answered Jesus.

He broke off a piece of bread, dipped it in a dish and handed it to Judas Iscariot. "Do what you have to do," he said. Judas Iscariot got up from the table and slipped quickly out of the room into the night.

Then Jesus picked up a loaf of bread and said a prayer to God. He broke up the bread and passed the pieces to the disciples.

"Eat this bread which is my body and remember me," he said. Then he picked up a cup of wine, said a prayer, and

handed it to the disciples. "This is my blood which I give for many people," he said. "Drink it and remember me."

When the supper was finished, Jesus and the disciples sang a hymn and then went out into the dark streets. They walked to a garden of olive trees, called Gethsemane. On the way, Jesus told his disciples that they would soon run away and leave him.

"I would rather die than do that," shouted Peter. Jesus said quietly to him, "I tell you that you will swear you do not know me three times before the cock crows at dawn tomorrow morning."

At Gethsemane, he asked some of the disciples to stay near the gates of the garden while he prayed to God. He walked away to a quiet place with Peter, James and John, and then went on alone to pray for the courage to face the terrible time that was coming.

When he went back to Peter, James and John, Jesus found they were fast asleep. "Couldn't you stay awake for just one hour?" he asked. "Please keep watch while I pray," and he walked away. After he had said his prayers, Jesus again went back to the three disciples and, again, they were asleep.

The third time Jesus woke up the disciples, they could hear loud voices and see torches flaring in the dark. It was the chief priests with the Temple guards. Judas Iscariot was leading them to where they could find and arrest Jesus.

Judas walked up to Jesus and kissed him on the cheek. "This is the man you want," he said to the guards. When the guards closed in, Peter drew his sword and tried to defend Jesus. He slashed off an ear of one of the High Priest's servants.

"Put down your sword," Jesus told Peter and, touching the man's ear, made it whole again.

The disciples were very frightened. They ran away, just as Jesus said they would. They left him alone to be marched by the guards back to Jerusalem.

Death on a Cross

Late that night, Jesus was taken by the Temple guards to the palace of Caiaphas, the High Priest. Many of the Jewish leaders were called there to put Jesus on trial.

Peter secretly followed Jesus through the streets to the palace courtyard. As he stood with some of the guards, warming himself by their fire, a servant girl walked past and looked at him. "You were with Jesus," she said. "I don't know what you mean," said Peter. Then another servant said, "This man was with Jesus." "I don't know him," swore Peter.

Later a man said, "You must know Jesus. I can tell you come from Galilee." Peter was very frightened. "I tell you, I don't know the man," he shouted. Then a cock crowed three times and Peter remembered that Jesus had told him he would deny knowing him.

127

Peter was so ashamed of himself, he ran out of the courtyard and into a dark corner, where he cried.

In the palace, the chief priests and the Jewish leaders began the trial of Jesus. They brought in many people who told lies about Jesus. But their stories did not match up. The leaders wanted to find an excuse to kill Jesus, but they couldn't prove he'd done anything wrong. All through the trial, Jesus said nothing and wouldn't answer any of the charges.

In the end, the High Priest asked Jesus if he was the Son of God. "I am," answered Jesus, quietly. "You heard what the prisoner said," the High Priest told the people there. "Do you find him guilty or not guilty of a crime against God?" "Guilty," shouted the people, and they hit Jesus and spat at him.

The High Priest sentenced Jesus, but before he could have Jesus put to death, he had to take him to Pontius Pilate, the Roman Governor. Only the Roman Governor could give the order for an execution.

When Judas heard that Jesus was to die, he was terribly

sorry he'd given Jesus away to the chief priests. He went to the Temple and threw down the thirty silver coins they'd given him. Then he went out and hanged himself.

In the morning, Jesus was taken to Pontius Pilate. The chief priests knew the Roman Governor wouldn't sentence a man to death for a crime against God, so they accused him of a crime against the Roman laws.

Jesus stood in front of the Roman Governor, who asked him questions but Jesus didn't reply. In the end, the Governor realized Jesus was innocent but he didn't want to make the Jewish leaders angry by setting him free.

At that time, it was the custom for the Roman rulers of the country to set one prisoner free at the Feast of the Passover. The people could choose who it would be. Pontius Pilate asked the crowd if he should free Barabbas, who was a murderer, or Jesus. The chief priests and Jewish leaders persuaded the crowd to ask for Barabbas.

"What shall I do with Jesus?" Pontius Pilate asked the people. "Crucify him, crucify him," they shouted. "What harm has he done?" asked Pontius. But the people just

shouted again, "Crucify him." Pontius turned away and washed his hands in a bowl of water to show that he was not to blame for Jesus' death.

Then he gave the order that Barabbas should be set free and Jesus was to be whipped before he was put to death. The guards took Jesus away and dressed him in a purple robe, pressed a crown made of thorns on his head and put a stick in his hand. They knelt in front of him, laughing and jeering. "Hail, King of the Jews," they mocked, beating him and spitting at him.

Then the guards dressed Jesus in his own clothes and made him carry a huge wooden cross through the streets of Jerusalem. Tired and weak from the beatings, Jesus stumbled and fell down again and again. At last, a soldier made a man called Simon, who was standing in the street watching, carry the cross for Jesus.

They led Jesus outside the city to a place called Golgotha. There the guards nailed Jesus' hands and feet to the cross.

They put a sign above his head which said, "Jesus of Nazareth. King of the Jews." Then they set up the cross between two other crosses. On them were thieves who had been sentenced to death. Jesus looked down at the soldiers and the people watching. "Forgive them, Father," he prayed. "They do not know what they are doing."

Some of Jesus' enemies were in the crowd. "If you really are the Son of God, come down from the cross. Then we'll believe you," they jeered. And the chief priests called, "You saved others, why don't you save yourself?"

Mary, Jesus' mother, was standing near the cross with John, one of the disciples. Jesus looked down at them. "Take care of her as if you were her son," he said to John. And from then on, John looked after Mary.

At noon, it grew strangely dark for about three hours. The crowd watched and waited in silence. At three o'clock, Jesus looked up and cried, "My God, why have you forgotten me?" Bowing his head, he said, "It is finished," and died. At that moment, the ground shook and the curtain in the Temple ripped from top to bottom. Many of the soldiers and the people were very frightened.

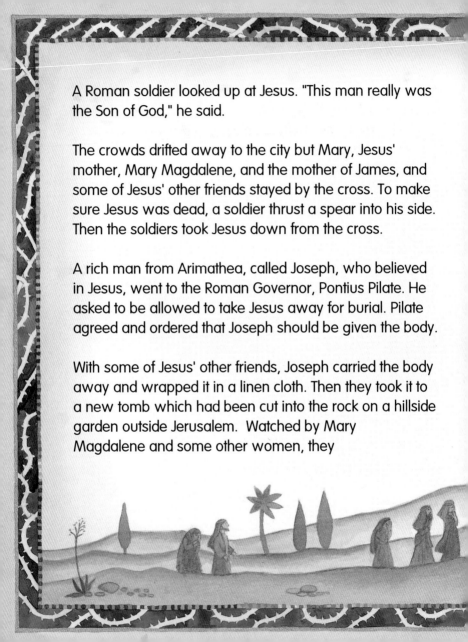

A Roman soldier looked up at Jesus. "This man really was the Son of God," he said.

The crowds drifted away to the city but Mary, Jesus' mother, Mary Magdalene, and the mother of James, and some of Jesus' other friends stayed by the cross. To make sure Jesus was dead, a soldier thrust a spear into his side. Then the soldiers took Jesus down from the cross.

A rich man from Arimathea, called Joseph, who believed in Jesus, went to the Roman Governor, Pontius Pilate. He asked to be allowed to take Jesus away for burial. Pilate agreed and ordered that Joseph should be given the body.

With some of Jesus' other friends, Joseph carried the body away and wrapped it in a linen cloth. Then they took it to a new tomb which had been cut into the rock on a hillside garden outside Jerusalem. Watched by Mary Magdalene and some other women, they laid the body in the tomb. Then they rolled a heavy stone in front of it, like a door, to close it. It was now Friday evening. The Jewish Sabbath begins at sunset and Jesus' friends had to leave the proper burial of Jesus until the Sabbath on Saturday was over.

The Jewish leaders asked Pontius Pilate to put a guard on the tomb. They were afraid someone might try to steal the body and claim that Jesus had come alive again. Pilate gave the order. His soldiers put a seal on the tomb and stood guard over it during the night.

The Empty Tomb

Very early on Sunday morning, Mary Magdalene and two women friends went to Jesus' tomb. They wanted to finish the preparations for the burial. They wondered how they would roll away the huge stone that blocked the entrance.

When the women reached the tomb, they were surprised to see that the stone had been rolled away and the soldiers guarding it had gone. A man in shining white clothes told them, "Jesus is not here. He is alive." When they looked into the tomb, they saw it was empty. The body was gone.

Puzzled and frightened, the three women ran to tell two

disciples, Peter and John. "They've taken the  Lord away," cried Mary, "and we don't know where they've laid him."

Peter and John ran to the tomb. John got there first, but didn't want to go in. When Peter came, he went straight in and saw the tomb was empty. But the cloths Jesus had been wrapped in were there. Peter and John didn't know if the body had been stolen or if Jesus had really come alive again. Very puzzled, they went quietly home.

Mary Magdalene went back to the tomb on her own. While she knelt, crying, outside the tomb, Jesus came and stood beside her. "Why are you crying?" he asked. "Who are you looking for?" Mary didn't look up. She thought it must be a gardener. "I'm crying because they have taken my Lord away. Please tell me where he is," she begged.

"Mary," said Jesus. Mary looked up and saw it was Jesus. "My Master," she cried. "Go and tell my friends you have seen me," said Jesus, "and that soon I will be with my Father in Heaven." Full of joy, Mary ran to tell the disciples that she had seen Jesus and that he had spoken to her.

On the Road to Emmaus

Later, on that Sunday evening, two of Jesus' friends were walking along the road from Jerusalem to the village of Emmaus. As they walked, they talked about Jesus.

Soon Jesus caught up with them and walked along with them. But they didn't recognize him and thought he was a stranger. "Why are you so sad?" he asked them.

"Are you the only stranger in all of Jerusalem who doesn't know what has happened there over the last few days?" asked one of the men, whose name was Cleopas.

"Why, what has happened?" asked the stranger.

"We are talking about Jesus of Nazareth," said the other man. "He was a great teacher. We believed he was sent by God to save our people. But the chief priests and our

Roman rulers said he broke the laws and must die. They nailed him to a cross last Friday and now he is dead. When some women went to his tomb today, they found that his body had gone. They said angels told them that Jesus is alive."

The stranger told them that the prophets had said all this would happen and explained it to them. At last, they reached Emmaus late in the evening. The stranger looked as if he would walk on, but the two men invited him to stay and have supper with them.

When they sat down to eat, the stranger picked up a loaf of bread, said a prayer, broke the bread into pieces and gave it to the two men. Then the two men knew that the stranger was Jesus. They stared at him for a moment and then he was gone.

Very excited, the two men got up from the table and ran all the way back to Jerusalem. They soon found the disciples and some of Jesus' other friends. They told them that they had seen Jesus, had spoken to him and that he was alive. At first, the disciples did not believe them but one said, "It must be true; Peter has seen him."

They locked the door of the room because they were afraid of the Roman rulers and chief priests. Then, suddenly, Jesus was in the room with them. At first, they were scared. They thought that he must be a ghost.

Jesus said, "Don't be afraid. Look at the wounds on my hands and feet. Touch me and see that I am made of flesh and bone." Then they knew that he really was Jesus.

"Have you anything to eat?" asked Jesus. They gave him some cooked fish and some honey comb and watched him eat it. At last, they were convinced that Jesus really was alive. He explained to them that this was all part of God's plan and that it had all been foretold by the prophets.

"Christ had to die and to come alive again on the third day," he said. "God forgives everyone who believes in Him. This is the message for all the people in the world and you must go and tell them."

Thomas, the doubter

Thomas, one of the disciples, was not with the others when they saw Jesus. He wouldn't believe it when they told him Jesus was alive. "I won't believe it until I see the marks of the nails on his hands and feet, and touch the wound in his side," he said.

A week later, Thomas was with the other disciples and the door of the room was locked. Suddenly, Jesus was with them again.

"Thomas," he said, "put your finger on the marks on my hands and on the wound in my side. Stop doubting and believe what you see."

Thomas didn't touch Jesus. He did not need to. "My Lord and my God," he said. "You now believe because you have seen me with your own eyes," said Jesus. "But more trusting are the people who have not seen me but still believe in me."

Breakfast by the Lake

During the next few weeks, Jesus' disciples and friends often saw him. One evening, Peter and some other disciples left Jerusalem and went to Lake Galilee. Peter said he wanted to go fishing. With the others, he stepped aboard a boat and they set sail across the lake. They fished all night but caught nothing. In the morning, when they were sailing back to the shore, they saw a man standing beside the lake. They didn't know it was Jesus.

"Have you caught any fish?" he called to them. "No, nothing," they shouted back.

"Throw your net over the right side of the ship," called Jesus. They did as he said and the net was soon so full of fish, they couldn't pull it in.

One of the disciples said, "It must be Jesus." Peter immediately jumped overboard and swam to the shore. The other men rowed the boat to the beach, dragging in the net bulging with fish. Jesus had lit a fire and he cooked some of the fish over it.

"Come and eat," said Jesus and gave them the cooked fish and some bread. No one dared asked him who he was but they all knew it was Jesus.

When they had finished eating, Jesus asked Peter, "Do you love me?" "You know I do," said Peter. Jesus asked Peter the same question two more times and each time Peter said he did love him. And each time, Jesus told him to take good care of his followers.

Wind and Fire

The last time his disciples saw Jesus was when they were walking on the Mount of Olives outside Jerusalem. He came to say goodbye.

"You must go back to Jerusalem," Jesus told them. "Wait there and soon God will send you the Holy Spirit. He will give you the power to speak bravely about me and all that I have taught you. You will speak to the people in Jerusalem and in many parts of the country, and even the whole world. Remember, I shall always be with you."

As the disciples watched, a cloud hid Jesus and he was taken up into Heaven. They looked up and saw two men dressed in white. "Jesus has gone to be with God but one day he will come back," they said.

The disciples went back to Jerusalem, feeling very happy, and waited as Jesus had told them. On the day of the Jewish festival of Pentecost, many of Jesus' friends, his mother Mary and some other women were with the disciples in a house in Jerusalem.

Suddenly, they heard noise like a great wind blowing through the room, but the air was still. Then fiery flames flickered around their heads but didn't burn them.

They knew this was the sign that God had sent his power to them. Now they could speak bravely to all people. The disciples rushed out into the streets of Jerusalem and told everyone they met about Jesus and the wonderful things he had done. They spoke in many different languages they had never learned so that everyone could understand them. The disciples told the people that they should be

baptized in the name of Jesus. They should be sorry for the bad things they had done, believe that Jesus died for them, and that God would always help them and be with them